TITANS
OF BUSINESS

RICHARD BRANSON

Dennis Fertig

Heinemann
LIBRARY

Chicago, Illinois

www.capstonepub.com
Visit our website to find out
more information about
Heinemann-Raintree books.

To order:

 ☎ Phone 800-747-4992

📠 Visit www.capstonepub.com
to browse our catalog and order online.

Edited by Mark Friedman, Nancy Dickmann,
   and Claire Throp
Designed by Richard Parker
Picture research by Liz Alexander
Original Illustrations © Capstone Global Library
   Ltd 2013
Illustrations by Darren Lingard
Originated by Capstone Global Library Ltd
Printed and bound in China by CTPS

16 15 14 13 12
10 9 8 7 6 5 4 3 2 1

Library of Congress Cataloging-in-Publication Data
Fertig, Dennis.
  Richard Branson / Dennis Fertig.
     p. cm.—(Titans of business)
  Includes bibliographical references and index.
  ISBN 978-1-4329-6429-0 (hb)—ISBN 978-1-4329-6436-8
(pb) 1. Branson, Richard. 2. Businesspeople—Great Britain—
Biography. 3. Virgin Group. I. Title.
  HC252.5.B73F47 2013
  338'.04092—dc23   2011050756
  [B]

Acknowledgments
We would like to thank the following for permission to
reproduce photographs: Alamy p. 19 (© Jinx Photography
Brands); Courtesy of Bishopsgate School p. 9; Corbis pp.
6 (© Hulton-Deutsch Collection), 23 (© Neal Preston),
24 (© James Leynse), 30 (© Stephen Hird/Reuters); Press
Association Images pp. 12 (PA Archive), 27 (Neil Munns/PA
Archive), 33 (Massimo Pinca/AP), 35 (Steve Parsons/PA Wire),
36 (John Stillwell/PA Archive), 37 (Andrew Parsons/PA Wire),
41 (Thierry Boccon-Gibod/AP); Reuters p. 39 (Mike Segar);
Rex Features pp. 11, 15 (Brian Moody), 13 (Bob Indge), 16
(Graham Harrison), 21 (Business Collection), 25 (O' Neil/Daily
Mail), 31 (Steve Bell), 32 (Per Lindgren), 34 (Stuart Atkins), 43
(Charles Sykes); Shutterstock pp. 5 (© stocklight), 7 (© Helga
Esteb), 29 (© Christopher Parypa); TopFoto p. 20 (Rik Walton:
ARENAPAL).

Cover photograph reproduced with permission of Getty
Images/Toby Canham (main image) and Shutterstock/© Eky
Studio (background image).

Every effort has been made to contact copyright holders
of any material reproduced in this book. Any omissions will
be rectified in subsequent printings if notice is given to the
publisher.

Disclaimer
All the Internet addresses (URLs) given in this book were
valid at the time of going to press. However, due to the
dynamic nature of the Internet, some addresses may have
changed, or sites may have changed or ceased to exist since
publication. While the author and publisher regret any
inconvenience this may cause readers, no responsibility for
any such changes can be accepted by either the author or
the publisher.

Contents

Find out what you need to do to have a successful career like Richard Branson.

Read what Richard Branson has said or what has been said about him.

Learn more about the people who influenced Richard Branson.

Discover more about the industry that Richard Branson works in.

Words printed in **bold** are explained in the glossary.

Introducing Richard Branson

As Ricky's family drove back from a vacation, he saw a sparkling river in the distance. Ricky begged his father to stop the car. Ricky wanted to swim in the river—or at least try. Earlier in the family vacation, Ricky's aunt bet him 10 **shillings** (worth about 8¢ in today's money) that he couldn't learn to swim. Five-year-old Ricky had done his best. But after two weeks of trying, he still couldn't swim. Now on the long drive home, Ricky was unhappy. He was afraid, but he had to swim!

His father pulled the car off the road. Ricky stripped down to his underpants and charged into the cold water. His family, including his aunt, calmly but alertly watched on the river's edge. Ricky struggled. But soon his struggles turned into the right strokes and kicks. He was swimming! When Ricky walked out of the water smiling, his aunt gave him the 10 shillings. Ricky also noticed that his dad was soaking wet. He had gone into the river, too, just in case.

From Ricky to Richard

Ricky grew up to be Richard Branson, one of the world's wealthiest **entrepreneurs**. The self-made billionaire runs 300 companies. He donates millions of dollars to charities. He has risked his life to set ballooning and boating records.

How did Branson achieve such success? The swimming story says it all. Branson didn't just risk his life for 10 shillings. He did it because he loved challenges and wanted to succeed.

Young Ricky grew up to be one of the richest people in the world.

An Interesting Childhood

Richard Branson was born in 1950 in Shamley Green, Surrey, in England. It's doubtful that his parents knew how special he would be. But their lives did provide strong hints that he would have a good life. His father, Ted, was a **barrister** (lawyer), as were Ted's father and grandfather. Ted hadn't really wanted to follow in their footsteps, but he was pressured into it. He wanted to be an **archaeologist**. But Ted's law career was successful—and so was his lifelong hobby of archaeology.

Branson's mother, Eve, was an athlete and professional dancer. When World War II began, she joined a **glider** club. The club taught future Royal Air Force (RAF—the British air force) pilots how to glide—a step toward becoming a pilot. As a woman, she wasn't allowed to be an RAF pilot or even a glider pilot. But she hid her long hair, faked a deep voice, and learned how to glide.

An RAF glider pilot in training over England, before heading off to combat in Western Europe.

Eventually Eve taught RAF recruits how to glide, too. After the war ended in 1945, she became an **air hostess**, a job for truly brave women in those days. Ted Branson knew how to win the heart of this risk taker. He proposed to her as they rode on a speeding motorcycle.

Ricky

Ricky was the oldest of three children. His childhood was often an adventure. His parents brought him up to be independent and strong. That's how little Ricky learned to swim!

Branson with his mother, Eve, in 2010 at a Virgin charity event.

"My mother was determined to make us independent. When I was four, she stopped the car a few miles from our house and made me find my own way home across the fields."

Richard Branson in his autobiography

Home and school

Branson's parents treated him and his two sisters as small adults. Their father's law cases and current events were dinner table topics. Their mother involved them in many entrepreneurial efforts. The most successful was making wooden tissue boxes that were sold at Harrods, London's famous department store. Branson wrote later that the tissue-box business became "a proper little **cottage industry**."

School was a more difficult challenge. At the age of eight, Branson was sent to a **boarding school** called Scaitcliffe. Students can live as well as study at a boarding school. Branson suffered from **dyslexia**. Dyslexia was not well understood in the 1950s. Teachers just thought Branson was stupid, or a troublemaker. The school tried to correct student behavior with **corporal punishment**. Richard was frequently punished, and almost **expelled**. But he survived. On his own, he also began to learn by working around his dyslexia.

Dyslexia—work around the challenges

Dyslexia is a disorder of the nervous system. A person with dyslexia finds it difficult to figure out and understand letters in words, or words in sentences. Dyslexia interferes with children's reading skills, but by adulthood most dyslexic people read as well as other adults. Dyslexia is not an intelligence problem. Many dyslexics have high **IQs**.

In the 1950s, few people knew much about dyslexia, or how to help children overcome it. Many children like Branson found their own ways to handle the challenge. He explained that he trained himself to concentrate to understand meanings of words and sentences. He also trusted his **intuition** to tell him what things meant. That's the first lesson of Branson's success: work your way around your challenges!

Branson's first school was Scaitcliffe (now called Bishopsgate), a boarding school in Englefield Green, Surrey, in England. When Branson was at Scaitcliffe, the school followed the tradition of the time and used corporal punishment.

Another school

When he was a teenager, Branson went to an all-boys school called Stowe. There, he discovered that, despite his dyslexia, he could write. He won a writing contest and improved in most subjects, except math and science. He was still far from being a perfect student. He protested against school rules and disliked the military training at Stowe.

During breaks from school, Branson followed his mother's entrepreneurial tendencies. With his friend Nik Powell, Branson started businesses. One was growing and selling Christmas trees. Another was raising and selling pet parakeets. Neither succeeded, but each taught him how to think about creating a business. It also showed Branson that he could handle real-life math, even if he was not very good at it at school.

A new idea

Back at Stowe, Branson's unhappiness with rules and regulations continued. The headmaster (principal) suggested that Branson write about it in the school magazine. Branson had another idea. With classmate Jonathan Gems, he planned to start a new magazine—but not just for Stowe. It would be a magazine for students at schools all over the United Kingdom. At the age of 15, Branson began developing *Student*. At 16, he left school to run the magazine full time. As Branson left Stowe, the headmaster told him, "I predict that you will either go to prison or become a millionaire."

"If I was calculating how much a Christmas tree would grow, or how many budgies [parakeets] would breed, the numbers then became real and I enjoyed using them. Inside the classroom, I was still a complete dunce [idiot] at math..."

Richard Branson in his autobiography

The boy who had trouble reading grew into a young man who founded a magazine.

A Good *Student*

Before Branson left school, he created a business plan for *Student*. He estimated the costs of starting the magazine and the possible **income** it could earn from sales and advertising. Branson also did something most teenagers or adults could not easily do. He fearlessly contacted well-known musicians, authors, and other celebrities and asked them for interviews—or even to write articles. He even wrote to 250 members of parliament, the British version of Congress.

After Branson left Stowe, he and Gems set up *Student's* office in Gems's parents' house in London. London was the heart of the art and music world in the 1960s. The two partners worked hard to get stories and advertisements ready for the first issue. *Student* was finally published in January 1968. Over the next few years, many of the famous people that Branson had asked for help gave interviews to *Student*. Branson himself interviewed rock stars such as John Lennon and Mick Jagger.

Branson at his desk, in *Student's* early days.

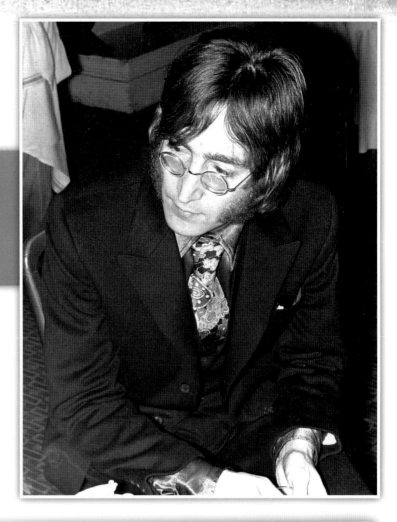

John Lennon, of the Beatles, was at the center of London's rock music world.

London in the late 1960s

In the early 1960s, American rock 'n' roll ruled the pop music world. Then, in 1963, a Liverpool band called the Beatles created fresh music that thrilled British teenagers. The Beatles repeated their success in the United States and led the "British Invasion" by rock bands such as the Rolling Stones and the Who.

The creativity in British rock encouraged creativity in other arts. By the late 1960s, London was a center of music and art **innovation**. Many musicians, artists, and businesses made money from British rock successes. Branson's **ventures** would benefit, too.

Success, then trouble

Initially, *Student* was a success. Many people read it. In 1968, the magazine moved to a real office and had a fairly large staff. Although *Student* never made a lot of money, Branson used some cash and his talents to found the Student Advisory Centre. The center gave free health advice to young people.

However, *Student* didn't bring in enough money. It began to fail. Branson had started *Student* because he wanted to be an **editor**. When it was in trouble, he focused on finding ways to keep the magazine alive. To his surprise, he found that he enjoyed the fight for *Student's* survival more than being its editor. Branson realized he was really an entrepreneur.

As *Student* struggled, Branson had a fresh entrepreneurial idea. This idea led to his first lasting success.

Never give up

How could someone who left school at 16 launch a national magazine? Three things helped Branson:

1. *He assumed he could do it.* Branson was too young to realize that getting famous people involved in *Student* might be impossible. He just did it!

2. *He found ways to get things done.* He got companies to buy advertising space in the magazine by telling them that their competitors were doing it. He worked out clever ways to limit costs, including the big expense of phone calls.

3. *He never gave up.* Branson worked long days, did brave things, and didn't accept the word "No." He made hundreds of phone calls, wrote hundreds of letters, and worked for many long hours.

Branson's long hours, hard work, and willingness to try new ideas helped *Student* become a real magazine.

Selling Music

Branson knew that young people bought records even when they couldn't afford them. He noticed something else, too. A new law allowed record stores to sell records at a **discount**, but no store did. Branson needed money for *Student* and the counseling center, so he ran an advertisement in *Student* for **mail-order** discount records.

How could such a young man own a mansion like The Manor?

The advertisement worked. *Student's* offices almost overflowed with orders and cash. Branson decided to develop a real mail-order record business. It was going to be called Slipped Disc, but someone suggested **Virgin** instead. This was because Branson and his young staff were inexperienced in business.

Branson's staff also promoted record sales by handing out leaflets where young people hung out. The leaflets worked better than the ad. Branson made a tough decision. He let *Student* die in order to focus on mail-order sales. As cash flew into Virgin Mail Order, Branson needed help handling finances. He asked his old friend Nik Powell to join him.

Virgin Records

In early 1971, post office workers went on **strike**. This wasn't good for a mail-order business. The strike led Branson to open a store where people could buy discount records. The store, called Virgin Records, was on Oxford Street in London. Branson designed it as a place where young people could hang out.

That same year, 21-year-old Branson also bought a 15-bedroom country mansion. He called it The Manor and started to change part of it into a musicians' **recording studio**.

"We wanted the Virgin Records shop to be an extension of *Student*; a place where people could meet and listen to records together."

Richard Branson in his autobiography

A hard lesson

In the spring of 1971, Virgin Records was crowded with customers and Virgin Mail Order had lots of orders. However, things seemed better than they were. The postal strike had hurt **profits**. Business costs were high. So were The Manor's **mortgage** and rebuilding costs. To control **expenses**, Branson did something he soon regretted. He cut costs by not paying taxes to the government. This was illegal. The police arrested him.

Branson spent one night in prison and had to pay a fine of £60,000 (almost $150,000 at that time). His parents loaned him the first £15,000. He had to pay the rest off over the following three years. Branson decided that the only way to do that was to open more record stores and make each one successful. The plan worked and ended Virgin's crisis. Three years after Branson was fined, Virgin was in good financial order.

Branson learned his lesson. He remembered his old headmaster's warning that he would either be a millionaire or a criminal. After his arrest, Branson carefully played by the rules. He didn't know if he'd be a millionaire, but he wouldn't be a criminal.

Getting a business on track

Virgin Mail Order seemed to do well. Orders came in and records were shipped out. But it wasn't that simple. Pretend you were Richard Branson. Do you know what costs you would have? The list is long: wages, warehouse rental, **utilities**, inventory (the records Virgin was trying to sell), shipping and mailing, advertising, **insurance**, interest on business loans, taxes, and more. Even someone as creative as Branson—or you—has to learn how to control costs.

In the 1960s, many people listened to music on record players like this one.

More stores, more music

As Branson opened more stores, he used three **strategies**. First, each store had to be friendly. Customers could linger, talk, and listen to music. Branson didn't expect them to buy something every time they visited. Second, he carefully chose store locations. He put them in areas that young people visited. The spots also had to have low rent. This was part of his cost-control battle.

The third strategy was a secret weapon: a young man named Simon Draper, who happened to be Branson's cousin. Draper was Virgin's music expert. He knew what music was being made, what was popular, and most importantly, what would become popular. Virgin Records didn't sell records that Draper didn't like—even hit records!

By the end of 1972, there were more than a dozen Virgin Records stores across the United Kingdom, and more coming. Branson had learned how to use profits from each new store to expand further. What was next?

Famous bands such as the Police (featuring Sting) often promoted their records at Virgin Records stores.

Simon Draper

Simon Draper came from South Africa. During his college days, he worked on a large newspaper, had his own radio program, and spent long nights listening to music. He knew the inner workings of rock songs and bands. He knew how a band's music changed from album to album, and why. He also understood how the political messages of some music affected listeners. Once he went to work at Virgin, he used his skills to predict and even set the tastes of rock fans. He made sure that Virgin stores had plenty of copies of the next big hit. Branson said Draper made Virgin stores "the hippest places to be."

Making Music

In the early 1970s, bands rented The Manor's recording studio to record music. **Record label** companies turned the recordings into records. Branson and Draper decided to start their own record label, Virgin Music.

Virgin Music followed several steps when creating a record. First it would sign up a band that Draper thought was good. The band borrowed money from Virgin Music to pay to use the studio. When the recording was done, the band had a record. Virgin Music then paid a factory to manufacture thousands of copies. Stores, including Virgin Records, sold the records. Branson's companies could earn a lot of money if the record was a hit. If not, they could lose money.

Virgin Music had great luck. Its first album, *Tubular Bells*, by musician Mike Oldfield, was a gigantic hit that sold millions of copies! At the age of 23, Branson had his greatest business success so far.

The haunting music of Mike Oldfield

By 1972, Mike Oldfield was a 19-year-old experienced musician who had made some recordings, but no hits. He spent much of that year and early 1973 living in The Manor and recording an instrumental album. He played about 20 different instruments, each of which had to be recorded separately. One instrument was a set of chimes called tubular bells, which became the name of the album. Virgin Music released the album in May 1973, and by August it was number one on the UK charts. That same year, *Tubular Bells* was used in the soundtrack of a hit film called *The Exorcist*. Worldwide sales earned Oldfield, Branson, and Virgin a lot of money.

Mike Oldfield played the guitar and many other instruments for his first Virgin Music recording.

Making music and money

For a long time, *Tubular Bells* continued to earn money for Virgin Music. But Branson learned how tough the music business was. He had to risk lots of money and make lots of records before there were other hits. Money earned by Oldfield's recording paid for many other failed recordings.

However, Branson was often motivated by love, not money. He loved music. So did Draper, who led the talent search. During the mid-1970s, the company had hits, but nothing like *Tubular Bells*. Plus, pop music had changed. Virgin Music's songs were considered old fashioned. Then, in 1977, Branson signed the Sex Pistols, a controversial **punk rock** band. Virgin Music's image quickly changed. Soon, even the world-famous Rolling Stones recorded at The Manor.

In the 1970s, Virgin Music introduced a new **logo**. Branson's business ideas and his companies were expanding. Eventually, the logo would appear on everything from mobile phones to spaceships.

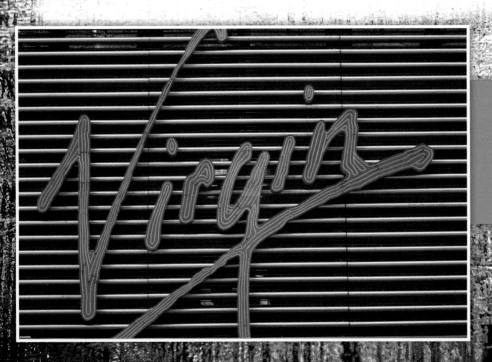

The Virgin logo is now among the best known in the world.

For many years, Richard Branson lived in and conducted business from a houseboat moored in a London canal.

How the music business has changed

Recorded music has been sold since the 1880s. The original technology used cylinders to record and play back sounds. Wax records quickly followed, and in 1906 the Victrola record player was introduced. When radio became popular in the 1920s, interest in records dipped. Radio sounded better. Eventually, recorded sound improved, and people bought records again. Records—now made of **vinyl**—were very popular when Virgin started. Then technology changed. Many people bought cassette tapes, not records. CDs replaced both in the 1980s. In the 2000s, Internet music downloads competed with CDs. With each change, people who made and sold music had to find new ways to profit.

Virgin Takes Off

The Virgin Islands were named by Christopher Columbus. It was there, Branson often says, that his airline business started. In 1978, Branson's scheduled flight from the Virgin Islands to Puerto Rico was canceled. Branson quickly **chartered** a plane. The plane was expensive for one passenger, so he made a sign that said "Virgin Airways: $39 Single Flight to Puerto Rico." He carried the sign around the airport. Soon the flight was full.

In 1984, an airline expert told Branson that more flights were needed between London and New York. Branson thought he could create an airline to meet that need. Many people doubted Branson could do it. Simon Draper feared the airline would hurt Virgin Music.

Branson spent months researching the airline business. He studied with many experts, including the legendary airline chief Freddie Laker. Eventually, he became an expert himself.

Sir Freddie Laker, airline revolutionary

Freddie Laker believed in competition. In 1966, he set up an airline called Skytrain that would offer regular, cheap flights between the United Kingdom and the United States. For 11 years, airline companies in both countries tried to stop him in court. They claimed that only they had the legal right to fly that route. In 1977, the courts took Laker's side, and his jets flew across the Atlantic. He cut costs and ticket prices. He was successful, until other airlines banded together and all cut their ticket prices below their costs. That was illegal, but Skytrain still went **bankrupt**. Laker sued those airlines for cheating and won again. His low-cost approach became a model for other new airlines.

Richard Branson honored Sir Freddie Laker by naming one of Virgin's largest airplanes "The Spirit of Sir Freddie."

Boom!

On June 19, 1984, Branson's new airline, Virgin Atlantic Airlines, had a test flight. The jumbo jet roared out of Gatwick airport in London with Branson and the entire airline staff on board. Suddenly—boom!—one of the jet's engines burst into flames! Quickly, the plane landed safely at Gatwick. Was this the end of Branson's latest dream?

No, it was still just the beginning. Two days later, the same plane had a new engine fitted. With Branson and his family and friends aboard, the plane flew smoothly to New York City.

Virgin Airlines not only succeeded, it made a profit in its first year. Today, Virgin also has direct or part ownership in other airlines, such as Virgin America and Virgin Australia. Virgin planes fly daily between the United Kingdom and United States, and to other places around the world.

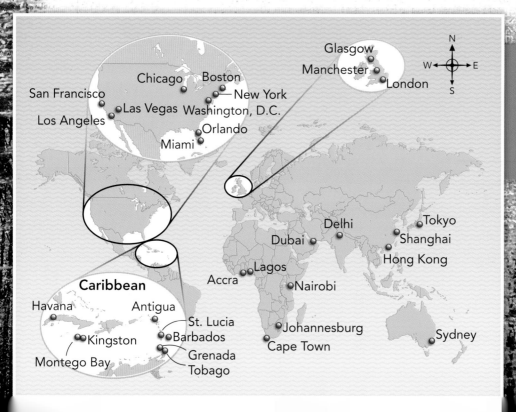

Virgin Airlines flies to places all over the world.

A big decision

However, Draper was right. Virgin Atlantic hurt the recording company. British Airways, the largest UK airline company, fought Branson for years. At times, British Airways even competed unfairly. For Branson, the costs of the competition and of running the airline were high, especially because he insisted on offering many onboard services to draw wealthy passengers.

In the early 1990s, the cost almost grounded Virgin Atlantic. The only way that Branson could save it was by selling Virgin Music and using the money to keep the airline flying. That sale broke his heart, but he knew when he started Virgin Atlantic that he was risking a lot.

Virgin America is one of Branson's new airlines.

"Don't worry, Richard. These things happen."
UK aviation official to Richard Branson after the engine blew out

Setting records

In the business world, Branson was a daredevil. Starting in 1984, he became a daredevil in a different way. He risked his life in attempts to set world records of various kinds.

The first was the fastest boat crossing of the Atlantic Ocean. Big ships had held the past records. In 1985, Branson and a crew tried it in a small powerboat. They were close to a record, when massive waves split the boat's **hull** and threw everyone into the raging sea! On his second attempt in 1986, Branson broke the record.

In 1987, Branson crossed the Atlantic in a gigantic hot-air balloon with **aeronaut** Per Linstrand. Seven other aeronauts had tried before. None succeeded, and five died. Branson almost drowned when the balloon dipped into the Irish Sea. However, the crossing was successful.

Yes, it is a boat and a car! Richard Branson used it to set a record.

Branson set other ballooning and sailing records. In 2004, he even crossed the English Channel in an **amphibious** car. He has also had failures. He tried three times to make around-the-world balloon trips without success.

A risk taker

Branson's adventures have earned great publicity for Virgin companies. His stunts were followed on television. Branson also believed his exploits gave Virgin employees the courage to make brave company decisions. Branson's willingness to accept risk is why he is a great entrepreneur.

Richard Branson (shown with actress Caterina Murino) played himself in the 2006 James Bond film *Casino Royale*.

Who is that guy?

Richard Branson's stunts have made him a celebrity. Because of that, he has been invited to make many television and film appearances. He often plays himself in comedies. On television chat shows, he is funny and charming. His appearances always provide publicity for his companies.

Virgin Multiplies

By the mid-1980s, Richard Branson had set up four main operations: Virgin Atlantic Airlines, Virgin Music, Virgin Records, and Virgin Vision (a company that produced and distributed films). But he was also adding more companies and splitting older ones into smaller chunks. For example, he eventually divided Virgin Records into a number of different companies, each with different interests and management.

One of these was Virgin Megastores, which sell records, videos, books, clothing, and more. Some new companies directly reflected Branson's personal interests, such as Virgin Airships & Balloons. Others appealed to him for purely entrepreneurial reasons, especially if he thought he spotted a fresh, profitable way to sell products or services.

Virgin Megastores were found in big cities around the world.

The world-famous logo and another Branson business float across the sky.

Branson still ran his business from a London houseboat, as he had done since the 1970s. Scattered across London were 25 buildings filled with Virgin companies and employees. Branson trusted and challenged the managers of each of his companies to make bold, independent decisions.

As the 1980s ended, The Virgin Group (as Branson's overall company was officially called) included over 150 companies in 20 countries. Together they made more than £626 million in yearly sales, which was just over $1 billion at the time.

Do you save your ideas?

Richard Branson always carries a notebook. He crams it with observations and ideas. In 1991, while visiting Japan, he rode on a speeding bullet train. He was deeply impressed by the Japanese rail system. He filled his notebook with thoughts about a British rail company. Later, he turned his ideas into a plan and his plan into a real railway.

Successes and failures

Branson has launched many businesses. Not all have worked out. In 1994, he introduced Virgin Cola. It didn't do well. Neither did Virgin Cinema movie theaters—nor Virgin Cars, an online auto company.

However, his successes far outnumber his failures. Virgin Mobile, a mobile phone service, and Virgin Active, a health-club chain based in South Africa and Europe, are recent triumphs. A surprising success is Virgin Limobike, a chauffeur service that uses motorcycles to move customers quickly through busy London traffic.

Virgin Limobike attracts many customers, including businesspeople and celebrities.

The Virgin brand

People think a **brand** is just the name of a product. That can be true. Many famous brands are tied to one kind of product. For example, Coca-Cola is known as a soft drink.

However, a brand can also be the *idea* of a company. Branson wrote in *Entrepreneur* magazine that the idea tells people what to expect. For example, he says the Virgin brand makes people expect that they'll be treated well, get a high-quality product at a good price, and also find some fun.

Everything that Branson does—stunts, television appearances, and founding new companies—helps to build that idea. The Virgin brand is so strong that other companies also want to use it. Branson will allow that, if a company meets his high standards.

An example is Virgin Balloon Flights. It existed under a different name, but it formed a financial partnership with Branson that allows it to use the Virgin brand. The company has to continually meet Virgin's high standards. It also has to treat customers well, provide a high-quality product at a good price, and offer some fun.

Going Green and Giving Back

In 2000, Branson was given a **knighthood** by the queen. He is now Sir Richard Branson. He also turned 50 and took a deeper look at the world. Branson's views led him to act in two different areas: improving the environment through entrepreneurial efforts, and improving people's lives through special Virgin programs.

Branson was once undecided about the reality of **global warming**. He no longer doubts this. He believes human activity causes warming or worsens it. He knows that his businesses—his planes, trains, and motorcycles—all produce greenhouse gases. He has pledged all the profits from Virgin airline companies to finding Earth-friendly fuels. He's convinced that for such fuels to be widely used, they have to cost less than oil-based fuels.

Richard Branson was knighted by the queen in 2000 and became Sir Richard Branson.

Helping the environment

Branson also thinks entrepreneurship might solve global warming. Through the Virgin Green Fund, he has been investing in companies that show great promise in finding successful and profitable ways to improve the environment. He has also set up the Virgin Earth Challenge. Virgin will award a $25 million prize to the inventor or company that can find a way to successfully remove greenhouse gases from Earth's atmosphere. Sadly, Branson knows there is a chance that there will be no winner.

Former U.S. Vice President Al Gore joins Richard Branson in announcing the Virgin Earth Challenge.

"What we're hoping to do is to actually come up with an alternative fuel that will shake the very foundations of the oil companies and coal companies—because if we don't shake their foundations, the world could potentially be doomed."

Richard Branson, to CBS News, 2007

Helping others

Branson founded the Student Advisory Centre in 1968 and has continued to try to help others. As he grew older, he had more money and time, so his involvement in charities grew.

Virgin Unite, founded in 2004, is the charity tool that Branson, Virgin employees, and others use to help the world. Virgin Unite grew out of the fight to prevent **HIV/AIDS**. It now includes the Elders, a group of 10 world leaders who work to stop violent conflicts within and between nations. Another part of Virgin Unite is the Branson Centre of Entrepreneurship in South Africa and the Caribbean.

The Branson Centre of Entrepreneurship is especially important to Branson. The center cannot teach its students how to have good business ideas. It can, however, teach them how to make a good idea work. It is another reflection of Branson's great belief that **free enterprise** can make the world a better place.

The beat goes on

Branson, of course, still creates companies: Virgin Racing, Virgin Money, Virgin Gaming, and Virgin Media, among others. Virgin Money amazes some people. How can a company that once sold rock-and-roll records now also be a bank? Branson doesn't see it as odd. Virgin Money provides a service just as Virgin Music did.

A new magazine

In 2010, 40 years after *Student* magazine died, Branson and his daughter Holly launched a new magazine called *Project*. The magazine is digital and only available for iPads. Its subjects cover some of the same subjects that *Student* once covered: musicians, artists, and writers. But it has one special addition: entrepreneurs.

Richard Branson wears a suit made out of an old technology, newspapers, to promote a new technology, a digital magazine. The launch of *Project* took place outside the Apple store in New York City.

Richard Branson Looks Upward

In July 2011, people around the world watched sadly as *Atlantis*, the last space shuttle, roared into the skies. A great, long chapter in space flight was ending. Many people wondered when another space vehicle would blast off from the United States. Richard Branson had the answer. He said: "It is possible, perhaps even likely, that Virgin Galactic's *SpaceShipTwo* will be the next vehicle to take humans into space from U.S. territory."

Virgin Galactic, based in the United States, may represent Branson's biggest dream. At first, though, the idea seemed like a publicity stunt. Was Branson really selling rides into space? It wasn't a stunt.

The designers of *SpaceShipOne* had won a $10 million prize for being the first company (not government) to build and send a real spaceship high above Earth. That's when Branson got involved. The *SpaceShipTwo* project appealed to him because it was an adventure, a moneymaking idea, and an attempt to aid Earth. Branson believes space exploration can help humans solve some of this planet's environmental problems.

Selling tickets to space

Virgin Galactic has spent a great deal of time and money developing and testing the world's first commercial spaceship. It can carry six passengers. Branson easily sold the seats on the first official flight. Tickets cost $200,000 each. He also has a waiting list of more than 400 people, who have paid $20,000 each just to get on the list.

There have been delays in the first launch. Still, the odds are that Branson will achieve that goal, too, and that he'll be on that first flight.

Want to bet 10 shillings?

Branson enjoys risking his life in daredevil stunts, but his business risks have brought him and others much larger rewards.

"Virgin has created more than 300 branded companies worldwide, employing approximately 50,000 people, in 30 countries. Global branded revenues in 2009 exceeded £11.5 billion (approx. US$18 billion)."

Virgin Group website

How to Become an Entrepreneur

Richard Branson became a successful entrepreneur because he was brave enough to put his ideas into practice. His story is filled with practical things that young entrepreneurs can try.

Find a great idea that helps people and fulfills a need
The magazine *Student* was intended to entertain and help students across the United Kingdom—and there wasn't a magazine like that in the 1960s. Virgin Records helped people buy records at discount prices—and no UK record shops were doing that at the time.

Respect people, and treat them well
Branson respects and enjoys people. He gets affection and respect in return. That makes everything else easier, no matter what problems occur in a business or life.

Value your ideas
Branson writes down his ideas. He may not use every one, but he values them enough to save and rethink them.

Be brave
Do not allow fear to stop you from trying your good ideas. Branson bravely contacted politicians, celebrities, and advertisers to make *Student* a success.

Have a plan
Remember the Christmas trees and parakeets? Work out how much a business will cost, and how much money it might make.

Be stubborn
At the age of five, Branson kept trying to learn to swim. When he was 34, he worked stubbornly to create Virgin Atlantic Airlines.

Do the impossible

At the age of 21, Branson bought a country mansion because he knew musicians needed a comfortable place to record music. People that young weren't supposed to be able to buy mansions.

Branson dresses in a full space suit to promote his new business venture, Virgin Galactic. He plans to do the impossible again and fly into space.

Glossary

aeronaut balloon pilot

air hostess female flight attendant

amphibious able to live or function on both land and water

archaeologist person who studies the people and customs of ancient times

bankrupt unable to pay off debts

barrister lawyer; person who can argue legal cases in the highest courts

boarding school school in which students also live

brand logo, name, and features of a business that make it special and make people recognize it

charter rent out a boat, plane, or other form of transportation

corporal punishment act of physically striking a person for a wrongdoing

cottage industry small business run out of a home

discount price reduction

dyslexia reading difficulty that occurs when a person has trouble recognizing letters or words

editor person who decides and prepares what will be in a magazine, newspaper, or book

entrepreneur person who takes financial risks to set up and run new businesses

expelled kicked out or removed from a school

expenses things that need to be bought or paid for to run a business

free enterprise system that allows businesses to develop and compete with each other without government control

glider aircraft that has no engine and floats on air currents

global warming increase in Earth's temperature

HIV/AIDS often fatal disease of the immune system that humans can pass to each other